To

_____

_____

_____

_____

From

_____

HEARTLIGHT
- Teach your child to shine

Gitte Winter Graugaard

The purpose of this book is not to give medical advice, nor to give a prescription for the use of any technique as a form of treatment for any physical, medical, psychological, or emotional condition.

The information in this book does not replace the advice of a physician, either directly or indirectly. It is intended only as general information and education. In the event that you use any of the information in this book for yourself, as is your constitutional right, the author and publisher assume no responsibility for your actions. No expressed or implied guarantee of the effect of use of any of the recommendations can be given. The author and publisher are not liable or responsible for any loss or damage allegedly arising from any information in this book.

Without limiting the rights under copyright reserved above, no part of this publication may be reproduced, stored in, or introduced into a retrieval system, or transmitted in any form or by any means (electronic, mechanical, photocopying, recording, or otherwise), without the prior written permission of the copyright owner.

The scanning, uploading, and distribution of this book via the Internet or any other means without the permission of the publisher is illegal and punishable by law.

Please purchase only authorized electronic or printed editions, and do not participate in or encourage any electronic piracy of copyrightable materials. Your support of the author's rights is appreciated. When you support a passionate soul you ignite her fire and help her change the world into a better place.

While the author has made every effort to provide accurate information regarding references and Internet addresses at the time of publication, the author does not assume responsibility for errors or changes that occur after publication. The author also does not assume any responsibility for third-party websites and/or their content.

Heartlight - Teach your child to shine © 2021 Gitte Winter Graugaard

Remember, we all arrived on this beautiful planet as light and love. You too. And we can always return to that place within ourselves if we have lost our way in life, if the darkness has penetrated our castle. We are light and love. Let it shine.

Gitte Winter Graugaard

Other books in English by Gitte Winter Graugaard:
The Children's Meditations In My Heart
Meet Chief Eaglefeather
The Flamedancers' Fire

More books will be available in
several languages in the future.
See where we're at with our words here:
www.gittewintergraugaard.dk

Heartlight - Teach your child to shine
Copyright © Gitte Winter Graugaard 2021
All rights reserved

Author: Gitte Winter Graugaard
Translation: Janny Marie Landegent Peterslund
Editor: Sam Jennings
Illustrations: Maria Tran Larsen
Layout: Katrine Høyer

1st edition
ISBN: 978-87-93210-59-2 (Paperback)
ISBN: 978-87-93210-38-7 (Hardcover)
ISBN: 978-87-93210-46-2 (ebook)
ISBN: 978-87-93210-37-0 (PDF)

Room for Reflection Publishing
www.gittewintergraugaard.dk

Contents

Foreword by Dr. Paul Luftenegger . . . . 7.

Introduction . . . . 11.

Five pieces of advice . . . . 13.

Let's meditate . . . . 16.

Choose an ending . . . . 57.

After the meditation . . . . 59.

Your notes . . . . 62.

About the author . . . . 70.

About Dr. Paul Luftenegger . . . . 72.

More from Gitte . . . . 74.

Foreword by
Dr. Paul Luftenegger

Multi award winning singer/songwriter/composer

I wish someone had read Gitte's books to me when I was a little boy because I know if they had, I would have been much more capable and much more equipped to navigate the world and the challenges it holds with more love and light and confidence from my own heart. It took me 34 years to begin to understand what Gitte has gifted you and your child with HEARTLIGHT.

Gitte's work has already changed the world forever in more than 20 countries and let me assure you, she is just getting started!

HEARTLIGHT is truly bursting with radiant love and light! This little powerful gem of a book is a gift to both you and your child, and it will do exactly as its title suggests, teach your child to shine. To shine from deep within their hearts, and to provide them with a tool with which to navigate the world, empowering them from the inside out.

This book will enable you to connect with your child like nothing else can. It will help you create a bond of trust between your heart and your child's heart that only a book like this can do. It will guide you with precision and great care to the delicate space of the heart we each have within us.

As an International (Canadian) multi award-winning singer/songwriter/composer, I write conscious, kind loving music to help the heart and soul feel its worth from within, and I know very well the power words and kindness can have when fused together with divine love from our hearts. I would never put my name to something unless I truly believed it would and could help the heart of the world with love.

In my global worldwide audience I experience the power of divine love from the heart every single day, and its majesty and magical power never ceases to amaze me! This book is filled with pure love and Gitte masterfully takes you into the holy space of the inside world of your child's body with care and kindness – the inner sanctuary of what is often referred to as the temple that houses the sacred heart and soul.

The word "core" came from the French word "coeur" – meaning literally "heart". I truly believe that the core of our being is in fact the heart and with this type of book your child will thrive with light from the core of their being. I believe that when the heart feels empowered to shine with love and peace and goodness, it is then that the world shifts.

If we want to thrive in our world, moving forward we must all heal our own hearts and true healing begins with us understanding the inner space with peace and power that is self-generated. What I know for sure is that the world heals when we ourselves are healed.

I love you Gitte, with all of my heart. Thank you for asking the little boy in me to be a HEARTLIGHT for your precious, precious book! Thank you for helping to heal the heart of the world with your HEARTLIGHT. You are very special and an important part of uniting the world from the sacred space of the heart.

All my love, in gratitude and grace,
Dr. Paul Luftenegger

www.beekindness.com

Introduction

I believe that all children are born full of light and love. But sadly that is not what I see when I walk into schoolyards and Kindergartens today. For many different reasons, too many children today find it necessary to dim their inner light from an early age. Too many children lose their connection with their hearts too early in life.

As adults who have access to our hearts, it is crucial we teach children that it is safe to glow, shine and share their beautiful inner light.

Let's remind our children that we all carry the most amazing light in our hearts and that we can turn up this light and increase its glow whenever we need to.

I wrote 'HEARTLIGHT' for my book 'The Monster Manual – for children who worry a lot'. However, as I sensed that many more children (and parents) needed this meditation, I decided to publish it as a standalone meditation too.

'HEARTLIGHT' is a children's meditation that draws on the practices discussed in my other book, 'The Children's Meditations in my Heart'.

With 'HEARTLIGHT' we take things to the next level and begin teaching our kids to work more intensively with the vibrations that our love and inner light bring forward. The meditation can be used across all age groups and certainly helps adults also. I recommend you begin when your child is 5 years old or older.

Through this children's meditation, you help your child to shift their focus from their minds to their bodies, and you teach the child to find inner strength and bravery in their hearts. This is so important.

Together we brighten the glow of the light and help the child spread it around their entire body. You can read it to your child when they need some peace of mind. It can be particularly useful at bedtime. It can also be put to use when wanting to remind your child about the powerful glow within their heart, when challenges are on the horizon.

It is nice to feel illuminated and get the sense of moving from darkness to light on the inside. For some, it can also have a healing effect on aches and muscle tightness as well as improving mental health. If you believe in the healing power of humans, this serves as a little introduction to your child.

My practice of teaching my own children to send the light from their heart towards an aching or sick part of their bodies has been a fantastic journey. Teaching them about healing from an early age, gives me a lot of hope for their futures.

I believe that when children grow up knowing about the strength they hold within their lion hearts and when they feel connected to their heart power, they will not only be able to find balance in life, but will also be able to live their lives to the fullest.

Five pieces of advice - if children's meditations is new to you

1. Delve into being present and find your love before you start. Breathe fully into your stomach and allow yourself the time to find peace. Your child will mirror your energy.

2. Pause throughout the meditation. I have marked places where I recommend a pause by means of three hearts. It may be your child needs more pauses. Give their imagination the time and space to explore.

3. Stay calm, even if your child is fidgeting. This is completely normal. Be patient with your child whilst they get used to a new practice of reading aloud

4. Notice whether your child sleeps faster, better and/or longer after the meditation. Pay attention.

5. Meditation opens the doors to creativity. Encourage your child to draw or write about their experiences with the meditation. Ask questions about the drawing and be curious about the insight your child gains through meditation.

Embrace the journey
Remember to enjoy this special moment of the heart with your child. It is the small intimate moments during your day - heart to heart, soul to soul - that create life's magic. These are the golden moments we hold in our hearts forever.

Begin with your eyes open and I will guide you into the meditation.

Five advices

Let's meditate

Dearest (insert name) _____

I am so happy for you and me. Today we get to find our inner light, turn it up and let it shine brightly. Doesn't that sound awesome?

When you were born your body was full of intense light and love. Try to imagine your body as a beautiful castle full of light. All chambers in your body were lit up by your soul celebrating a new and exciting life on planet Earth. You were shining so brightly it completely melted the hearts of the people who got to see you first. Mine included.

When your chambers are full of light it means that you are connected to your true power, your pure essence and you feel immense love inside of you, which gives you courage, strength and lots of joy. However, as we begin to live our lives, for many often unknown reasons, we begin to let the light in some of the chambers dim and we no longer shine as brightly. Some chambers we dim ourselves with feelings of embarrassment, shame or guilt. Other lights we let other people dim through harassment, belittling, mockery or even worse, violence and physical or mental attack.

So little by little, some of the chambers within our beautiful castle are dimmed and in time, even forgotten, locked up - the key thrown away with a 'do not enter' sign hanging from the handle. Maybe you recognise that feeling in your own body. Maybe you can even picture which parts of your body are darker than others.

Walking around with dimmed chambers inside of us isn't fun and can be quite challenging. This is why a children's meditation like this one is so amazing and so liberating.

When you close your eyes and breathe deeply into your stomach, you can access your inner world. Your imagination shows you the way.

The light comes from our hearts and in the meditations, we can go on a tour inside our inner castle and relight the chambers we are ready to reopen, dust them off and let them shine again. The more rooms we let shine, the brighter we get, the lighter we become and the more fun we attract.

When closing your eyes and opening up to your imagination, you can move the light of your heart through your body and use it to light up the dark chambers.

This allows you to feel better in the parts of your body where darkness hides. It will give you a feeling of being better able to find your way through the darkness, even when you are scared, sad or frustrated.

You, my friend, have the most beautiful inner light that I know of. I have seen it many times when you feel joyful. To me nothing is as beautiful as seeing the light of people's hearts in their eyes. Right there we get a glimpse of each other's souls

Are you ready to brighten the glow of your heart's light and spread it through your entire body?

Come, let's find your strength, your courage and your inner protective armour. I know that you are strong, much stronger than you even realise. In the light you will find your strength.

The light of your heart shines the brightest when your mind is at peace. So try to find your inner peace. It is time to sit or lie down comfortably. As you please.

Pull up a blanket or duvet and make sure you are lying or sitting comfortably and cosily. Relax your body and start breathing as deep down into your stomach as you can.

Try to breathe calmly in and out through your nose or in through your nose out through your mouth. Take deep breaths.

♡ ♡ ♡ (pause)

If you want to, you can close your eyes. If you aren't quite ready to do so yet, you can fix your gaze on a point in this room until you feel like letting your eyelids close softly. When you close your beautiful eyes, you will gain access to all the strength and beauty inside of you. Let your imagination open itself up to you.

The reason why meditation works well with children is because they have better access to their imagination than most adults.

♡ ♡ ♡

Notice the sounds you hear around us. Sounds far away and close by. Maybe you can hear your stomach rumble or the sound of your breath.

Now, just let the sounds be sounds and focus more and more on my voice and the images and emotions you may begin to see, feel or otherwise notice inside your body.

Sense your own breathing. Relax your body. Try to breathe all the way down into your stomach. Place a hand on the lower part of your stomach and when it moves up and down, you are ready to find your heart's light.

Imagine you are standing in a green meadow in a beautiful valley surrounded by the most beautiful mountains you've ever seen.

The sun is shining from a clear blue sky and there is no wind. It is not too hot, nor too cold. It is exactly the way you like it best.

You have bare feet and can feel the grass tickling them gently. A pleasant smell of summer is coming your way from the flowers, the grass and the trees around you. It is as if they are all welcoming you to this place. As if they know that someone very special has arrived.

In the background, you can hear birds and the most gracious little grasshoppers singing in a choir.

And look how nicely a little butterfly next to you flies from one flower to the next. Look at the marvellous colours of its wings; they are the most beautiful colours you know.

Sense how it feels to stand right here and feel entirely safe in your inner meadow. You will always be safe here.

The sun shines its golden rays across the sky. Just like you shine when you smile and feel joyful. When we look at the sun, it can remind us that we too are little suns, carrying the light inside of us.

We are all bearers of light, and if we remember that and know about the inner meadow you now stand in, we can come back again and again to turn up the lights in our hearts, letting it spread into all the chambers of our bodies whenever we need to.

Now imagine a beautiful mountain in front of you. The most magnificent mountain you have ever seen. It is your mountain of love and it is calling for you. Can you hear it calling your name?

Your heart lives inside that mountain. Let's go find it. When you find your heart, you will also find your heart's light and in that, your inner strength. Are you ready to go see the light? Just give me a little sign with your hand or your foot and we will enter your love mountain together.

At the foot of the mountain, you see a large and heavy wooden door. Although it is heavy and protective, it opens as easily as anything when it sees you coming toward it. The mountain recognises you and loves when you come to visit to turn up the light of your heart.

♡ ♡ ♡

As you enter you are standing in the beautiful entrance to your heart chamber. You are met by a sea of light, shining in the most magnificent colours. Try to see the light from your heart now.

♡ ♡ ♡

Maybe you also hear some lovely sounds. Listen carefully. Those tunes are the music of your heart. You might also hear your heartbeat.

♡ ♡ ♡

We often get the feeling of coming home when we get connected to our hearts. The heart is our safe space to find peace, comfort and light, no matter where we are or what we are experiencing.

Right here inside the mountain you get as close to your source of light as possible and that feeling resembles the feeling we come with when we are born, a feeling of being full of light and love.

As long as you are alive, and your heart is still beating, it will be full of light. Sometimes we just forget. So now that you know about the light in your heart and also how to connect to it, you are a very lucky child.

Look around in the chamber of your heart. What do you see?

What do you feel?

What do you hear?

Is there a smell here or even a taste?

Apply all your senses.

As you go further into your mountain, you see your big beautiful heart.

And you now clearly see there is an amazing bright light in the chamber that comes beaming from your heart. It is the light of your heart that shines so brilliantly into the heart chamber and from there, into your body.

Look at how fine and magical your heart's light is. Maybe you see the light, maybe you sense it. Look at and feel how much love you hold inside of yourself. And look at how brightly you shine. Feel how brightly you shine.

♡ ♡ ♡

You are the light. You are love.

Let's see if you can turn up your love and in doing so, brighten the light of your heart even more, so that it shines into the chambers of your body that need light.

Let's imagine that there is a dial in the middle of your heart. When we turn it up you fill your heart with even more love and with that love, you brighten the glow of your inner light. Try turning it up! Think about all the things you love to do, the people you love and the love you have for yourself, and turn up that love even more.

It's like the feeling of a hug that gets better and better.

No matter how your day has been, you can always enter your heart chamber and brighten the glow of your heart by turning up your love for yourself, for those around you and for life itself. And I know you have lots of love inside of you. I often see it and feel it.

And I am forever grateful I get to be with you on both the days when you shine brightly and on the days when you need to go to the mountain to top up your heart, head and body with light and love again. I always love you.

There'll be days when you'll need to turn it up more than normal. If you have had one of those days where darkness has stolen into your thoughts and crept into your body, it can be very helpful to turn the light up as bright as it will go, spreading it into the parts of your body where it is needed the most.

It is a little like turning on a flashlight in a dark room, finding the switch, turning on the light, opening the curtains and the windows and letting in the sun and fresh air.

It could be the chamber then needs a little cleaning. You will know what to do in each chamber if you use your imagination and allow yourself to be guided.

When we light our inner light it becomes easier to find our way out of the darkness. Remember, that even on the darkest of days, you still carry the light inside. Find your way to that light, turn it up and spread it out.

Let's meditate

Next to your feet you see a long piece of magical fabric folded on a little golden tray. The fabric shines in beautiful golden colours. It is your golden cape lying there. It is woven from gold extracted from the purity of the golden light shining from your heart. As gold is made of metal, it can protect us like an inner golden armour.

Now try picking up the cape and carefully tie it around your shoulders. I am sure it fits you perfectly. It is your cape after all.

When you were very young it was smaller, and since you have grown bigger it has grown with you. And in a bit, when you go out and spread your light throughout all of your body, the cape will leave a fine golden web behind it.

This web will settle everywhere in your body and give you protection and inner strength.

Notice how the cape gives you strength, hope and courage already. It is as if it shines even brighter now that you are wearing it and are preparing to be the Light Bearer of your HEARTLIGHT.

If all the people of the world knew how to do, what you're about to do, and did this every night before they went to sleep, we would be able to create peace on Earth. And in a moment, when you bring the light out into your body, your body will feel peaceful. This is how peace in the world begins: child by child, adult by adult – as we all become the Light Bearers of our own light.

When we let ourselves shine, we remind those we meet on our way that they too, can shine. When we shine, peace comes to us. People around us can feel that. As more and more people carry the light from their hearts out into the world and make peace by means of the most magnificent thing we possess – namely our love – we begin to heal, and when we heal we can heal the planet as well.

Are you ready to be a bearer of the light? I know you have it in you, because I have seen you use it many times before. And now that you are familiar with the light of your heart and you carry your golden cape, you will only get braver still.

To bring the light of your heart with you, you must carry it. So, hold out your hands in front of you, joining your little fingers so that you form a little bowl with your hands. Bring the bowl over to the light in the middle of your heart, to the place where it shines the brightest, and let a little ball of light land in your hands.

Sense how lovely it feels when the light of the heart touches your hands. It is the softest thing you have ever felt.

Fill your hands with a shining ball of light and carry it along with you like a torch.

With the cape around your shoulders and the ball of light in your hands, you now examine the chamber.

Imagine seeing four different exits located around the chamber: one at the top, one at the bottom and one on either side. The top exit leads to your head and the bottom exit leads to your stomach and legs, while your shoulders and arms are reached by the side exits.

Spend a bit of time imagining the four exits. What do they look like? How far are they from you? Sense that they have already been lit up by the light of your heart here inside your heart chamber.

Carrying your heart's light in your hands, you're ready to go exploring your body from the inside, spreading your light. Let's go.

The first exit you visit leads to one of your shoulders. You can now decide which arm you want to go to first. Imagine you are walking from your heart chamber with the light in your hands and walk through the exit leading to your shoulder and towards your arm. Carry the light towards your shoulder and light up everything on your way, bringing light to your chest and lungs too.

Watch the light spread through your lungs and your chest.

Imagine that each and every one of the millions of cells within your body light up wherever you go with the fine light of your heart.

♡ ♡ ♡

See how the light of the cells makes a beautiful sea of light around you. Pause a moment if you sense that some areas you pass through need some more light.

♡ ♡ ♡

It is often related to the places in your body where you sense a kind of pain, ache or discomfort. Or it can be in a spot where you hurt yourself and have a scratch or a bruise. It can also be around a body part you may not like so much and maybe even feel shameful about. Shame dims our light so fast.

When you light up these spots of darkness from within, you are helping your body to heal itself and ease the pain or discomfort. Just as we need light to see in the dark, your cells need light, love and happiness to become strong, resilient and healthy.

Imagine that your golden cape leaves a fine golden web trailing behind it and that this web settles as a thin cover along the path you tread, spreading all through your body. The web is so fine that you almost can't see it with the naked eye, but you can feel it. Because it protects you and provides strength.

Carry the light further into your shoulder, down through your upper arm and let the golden web flow behind you.

Spread the light into your elbow. Shine the light onto the bones of your arm too. Then try to light up the inside of your bones and let the web settle as a protective sheath around them. Shine your light into your muscles and ligaments.

Bring the light into your hands and drag the web behind you. Now your hands are shining even brighter.

Everywhere you go with the light of your heart, you are finding little switches in more chambers of your inner castle; you are relighting your soul's beauty, pulling the web behind you so that it envelopes so softly around you, protecting you.

When you reach your hands and fingers and the light begins to shine in your hands, they might become warmer too. Can you feel it? This is healing energy.

Sometimes, our hands shine so much with HEARTLIGHT, that we can feel it when we touch one another. Think about a long warm hug that grows in intensity or holding a hand you don't want to let go of. That is us sharing our light and love with each other. The finest gift we can give each other. Animals do it too and even the plants. It is all about energy.

Holding your HEARTLIGHT in your hands is magical. It is pure love shining from your hands. When you place a shining hand on body parts that hurt, on either your own body or another's, it feels very comforting.

So, if a specific area in your body is hurting right now, you can place your hand on the part of you that hurts, and bring light and love where your body needs it most.

Now go back through your arm, shoulder and chest into your heart chamber, carrying your ball of light in your hands still. And notice how you have lit up the entire path along the way.

Once back in your heart chamber, you can fill up the bowl you made with your hands with more light. Now it is time for the other shoulder to have an inner shower of light.

Drag the golden web behind you and go towards the opposite exit.

Carry the light and the web through your lung and chest. Shine your light as you walk the paths. Shine it into the cells and onto your bones. Shine it onto everything you encounter in your path.

Go to your shoulder, continue down through your upper arm, your elbow, your lower arm, your hands and your fingers and drag the golden web, the courage and the strength behind you.

Shine, shine, shine, my beautiful Light Bearer! Spread your love and light all through your body.

Once you have lit up your entire arm and have dragged the web behind you, you return to your heart chamber again. There you fill up your bowl with more light and then you go towards the top exit leading to your head. Now you reach your neck, which loves the light of the heart too. Your neck can be very sore if you have a lot to worry about and the heart's light can loosen up this soreness.

If your neck is feeling sore you can place your hands exactly where you feel the soreness. The light of the heart will pour out of your hands into your neck and help your body find balance and peace.

Relax your body as well and remember to breathe into your stomach. Let go of the darkness, let go of the tension, let go of the hurting.

Now shine the light of your heart into your throat and breathe deeply at the same time. Let the light mix with the air running down through your throat, your stomach. Light up the air.

Continue up into your head and shine your light onto your buzzing thoughts. Our brain is the place from where much of our darkness emanates and for this reason, our head often needs a lot of light from our hearts in order to heal.

Shining the heart's light inside of our heads gives us a brighter and lighter mind.

When we let the light of our heart spread throughout our head, we can see and experience it in each other in different ways.

Firstly, we can see it in the eyes. The light of the heart makes people smile with their eyes and often lets the eyes sparkle like stars. Especially in children. Exactly like I have often seen it in your eyes. I love seeing your heart's light in your eyes, it is one of the finest things I know.

The light of the heart also makes sounds seem more beautiful to the ears, exactly as music often sounds more beautiful when we are happy.

It also makes our voices become brighter, more beautiful and softer. The brightest sound I know is children's laughter. It sounds like music from the heart. Nothing in the world is as bright to me as your laughter.

And when our voices are lit up, brighter words come out of our mouths. Because the words, too, are filled with light.

It is so important to fill our heads with heartlight. Exactly like you are doing now; you are spreading a fine, golden web throughout the chambers of your head too. Carry on for just a little longer.

Being a Light Bearer and spreading your light into your head you now wear a crown of light on your head. Try to shine your light into your crown and notice how magnificent it is.

It lights up the room around you and connects you to the light of the Universe.

When you are ready, you can go back to your heart chamber and fill up your bowl with light again. On the way back, notice how your head, your neck and your shoulders are lighter.

You are so bright and beautiful.

All your cells are shining; they are smiling at you and they greet you as you walk past them. If you listen closely you can hear them humming as well. They thank you for coming, for shining on them.

They truly see you as the Light Bearer who can lead them out of darkness. To them you are a hero right now for turning up your light and letting it shine so beautifully.

Let's meditate

Back in your heart's chamber, you fill up your bowl of light again, and you see that the cape is still trailing behind you, spreading its golden web, as you walk towards the lower exit, the one that runs down into your lower body. It is the last of the four exits.

Let us start by spreading light into the solar plexus, which is the chamber directly under the ribs in the middle of your chest. Did you know, solar plexus means our inner sun? When we are happy, our solar plexus is at peace and balanced, and when full of light it beams light out of our bodies.

When we are sad, nervous, scared or we feel down, our solar plexus easily cramps up into a tight little knot. Some kids feel this cramping as something hard, or it can feel like being hit in the stomach. If you know that feeling, you are not alone and please know that it is not dangerous to feel this way.

Let me teach you how you can loosen up the knot using the light of your heart and your breath.

So let's try to make the knot relax, become soft and more elastic. Imagine the hard, little knot and how, slowly, you can massage it and start to shape it like a sort of play dough.

To begin with the knot is a bit hard and stiff, but with your warm, shining hands it is as if you can loosen it up so that it becomes soft again. See if you can massage it for a bit.

See if you can guide your light into the chamber of your solar plexus.

Your breath also helps you loosen up the knot. See if you can breathe into the chamber. Breathe into your solar plexus and spread your light.

When the knot becomes softer, it gets weaker and lighter and allows the golden web to enter and make your solar plexus stronger. When you let the light into your solar plexus, you might get fewer stomach aches and maybe you will also feel less sick. Shining the heart's light into the solar plexus is so powerful. However, sometimes we need to practise new skills.

Breathe and spend a bit of time filling this chamber of your body with light. Spread your golden web, so that you become strong and get the courage to do the things you want to do.

Once you're done, you can fill your stomach with light in the same way. If there are other places in your stomach where you often feel pain, it is especially nice to shine your light a little deeper into those places. And remember, if ever you need it, you can always go back and get more light from within your heart chamber.

Place your shining hands wherever you may hurt.

Continue further down when you are ready. Pause at your bellybutton and shine your light there. There is another amazing and important chamber, called Hara, just below your belly. See if you can find it and light it up.

And then continue to the lowest part of your upper body which we call our root. Light up that chamber too.

When you are ready, you can light up all of your spine; every part of your spine, all the way from your root to your head. Imagine you are lighting every bone of your spine as you go. All the way up, like lighting street lamps on a dark road. Oh, how you shine!

Notice how it feels. Maybe you feel like moving around a bit and that is perfectly fine. It is the energy that wants to spread. Let go of the darkness.

♡ ♡ ♡

Now go to your legs. First go into your one thigh, your knee and lower leg. Carry the light of the heart and your golden web through your entire leg and let it shine all the way into your little toe.

See how brightly you light up your path.

And now go to the other leg, the thigh, the knee, the lower leg and all the way to your little toe. Shine lots of light and love through your leg.

It is a little like getting an inner shower of light and love. And be grateful that you know this inner power is inside of you. Your greatest power comes from your heart. You carry a massive strength inside of you.

Now, you have illuminated your entire body. As you look down upon your feet you see that your light is spreading into the ground into Mother Earth. When you light her up, she sees you immediately and empowers your light with hers.

She loves to see little Light Bearers from near and far and always wants to help us.

Maybe you can feel the energy she sends to your feet right now.

Feeling connected to her makes you even stronger.

She creates the powerful waves of the ocean that can help you create flow, she can make fire in her volcanoes that can help you light your inner fire, she breathes air into your lungs through her forests and has given us a sky to dream into and to lift us up.

She is the solid foundation below us that grounds us and helps us create a home and learn new skills. All of her wisdom she lends to you right now through her light.

Receive it, embody it and say thank you.

Also notice how the light from the Universe comes down through your crown on top of your head.

The Universe salutes you for and supports you in your inner light work.

It is time to return to your heart chamber.

Carefully, you place the ball of light back into the light of the heart. As you do so, you notice how it melts into all the other light of the eternal source of light in your heart. It never runs out. In fact it is quite magical - the more light we spread, the more light we get.

At the foot of your heart, you put the cape back onto the little golden tray, so that you can easily find it again the next time you need more heartlight.

Before you go toward the door, you stand in front of the light of your heart and feel your gratitude for being in such close contact with your heart and your light.

When we show our gratitude, our heart's light shines even brighter and reminds us that we can always come back, seek the light of our heart, brighten its glow and spread it throughout our entire bodies.

You take a moment to look at the bright light of your heart; you feel, sense and appreciate the emotion before you return to the door.

The golden web you have spread throughout your entire body has left a fine, strengthening layer, which will protect you and give you courage and strength on your way forward.

See how brightly you shine. You are like a little sun. The light in you is so strong now, that all of us who meet you can see it from far away.

When you are back in the meadow at the foot of the love mountain, you are not sure who shines the brightest: you or the sun!

And the sun is so happy that it is making somersaults in the sky when it sees you.

Because just as we love the sun and its light makes us happy, the sun loves it when we people fill themselves with light and shine like little suns on Earth, into Mother Earth and to each other.

In this way, we who shine can go into the world together and spread the light of our hearts, our inner peace and calm. We spread our light first to ourselves and then to those who are lucky enough to meet us on our way. Beam your light and share it with those who need it. Thank you for shining so brightly.

And the next time you meet a child with shining eyes, you know that you are seeing the light of the child's heart. Cherish such a friend. Because then you also know that you have found another Light Bearer who can go on quests with you to spread even more light. Light Bearers are amazing friends.

Let their light remind you that you too are a Light Bearer. Seek those who shine and shine even brighter together on those who need your light to remind them that they too are light and love. Remember those who are hardest to reach need light the most.

That is how we change this world and create a better tomorrow - together. Thank you for shining your light.

Ending – choose the one that fits.

Nap or nighttime: With this beautiful inner shower of light, you are ready to enter the world of sleep and have beautiful bright dreams. Your sleep will help you cleanse even more.

Thank you for letting me come along on your inner light journey.

Sleep well, my shining Light Bearer.

Daytime: With this beautiful inner shower of light, you are ready to continue your day and shine like the little sun you are.
Thank you for letting me come along on your inner light journey and letting me see the beautiful light of your heart.

Now it is time to slowly and calmly return to this room. Start by moving your fingers and toes.

Sit up nice and slowly when you are ready, open your eyes.

Welcome back, my shining Light Bearer.

After the meditation

In the days after the meditation I recommend that you talk to your child about their experiences with this meditation. Some children are very visual and will have experienced the light journey through their bodies like a little movie perhaps, while others are more kinaesthetic and will have felt their way through. Support the sensory language that your child uses to express themselves, and ask about the things your child tells you.

It can be a very fulfilling and moving experience to draw the inner light adventure with your child. Often the creative expression after a meditation holds such gems; it can open up our subconscious, imagination, inspiration and playfulness.

Please also tune into your own light and see if you too need to fill your body with light. If your child is old enough to read the meditation to you, that would be a beautiful thing to do for both of you.

I have included a Notes section, if you feel like writing about some of your or your child's experiences with this meditation. These notes and observations could become of great value to your child later in life.

After meditation

Make some notes about your own or your child's experience with the meditation

Notes

Notes

Notes

When are you a Light Bearer?

How do you feel or see your own light?

You can draw what you saw in your meditation

Drawings

Drawings

About the Author

Gitte Winter Graugaard (b. 1977) is passionate about writing books that strengthen children's imaginations, as well as nurture their intuition and helping them balance life. HEARTLIGHT will be a gift to both you as the narrator and your child as children are in much better contact with their heart than adults and can teach us a lot about love if we listen! So be open to turning up your own light too.

Gitte holds a Masters Degree in Business Administration and has worked in communication, specialising in storytelling. She is also a trained Life Mastery Coach, Heartcore Mentor, Mindfulness Instructor and Conscious Transformer. In 2019 Gitte gave a passioned TEDx speech in England about helping children to sleep by being present as a parent. We recommend that you to watch it here:

www.gittewintergraugaard.dk/tedx

However, her most important knowledge about the beautiful art of listening to her heart, comes from Gitte's own life, which is filled with love and heart choice.

About the author

On the pages after the meditation, you can write notes about your own and your child's comments on their heartlight meditation experiences. We also recommend that you encourage your child to draw. Children's drawings often provide a great opportunity for a good conversation.

Together, let us fill homes all over the world with the most beautiful heartlight, created by love to and from our children.

Dr. Paul Luftenegger - a shared mission for love

When I first heard Paul sing "My Heart", my heart stood still. It felt like that song was sung from the soul of my book "The Children's Meditations In My Heart". Paul has a unique ability to heal while singing. His divine music is for good reason played at delivery rooms, nurseries, kindergartens, schools, hospitals among other.

I often play Paul's music when I teach kids meditation. He and I share a deep desire to help children thrive. In many ways I see Paul as the little Light Bearer on the cover of HEARTLIGHT. He brings out the child in us. From that beautiful place in all of us peace can grow. Thank you Paul, for your beautiful foreword in this book and for being my friend, together we create miracles.

My top favorite songs for children among Paul's many songs are:
"My Heart" from the album: Love expanding love
"Universal Love" from the album: Diamond Light
"Highest Self" from the album: Spheres of love
"The Miracle of you" from the album: The Miracle of you
"Beautiful day" from the album: Seeds of Peace
"Superman" from the album: Faith
"Spheres of Love" from the album: Spheres of Love.

About Dr. Paul Luftenegger

You can find Paul's music on all major streaming platforms.

A Global Mission

Gitte Winter Graugaard is on a mission to help ONE MILLION CHILDREN and their families fill their hearts with love at bedtime. She is an expert in peaceful bedtime routines. She is a bestselling and award-winning author, and a TEDx speaker.

Her books are helping thousands of children to sleep in more than 20 countries. Gitte always reminds us to parent ourselves first before we parent our children and become aware of what we radiate.

To find more inspiration to conscious parenting and better sleep, you can follow Gitte's blog on:

www.gittewintergraugaard.dk

To book Gitte for speaking or workshops go to:

www.gittewintergraugaard.com

Gitte talking at TEDx Peterborough UK, April 2019

More from Gitte

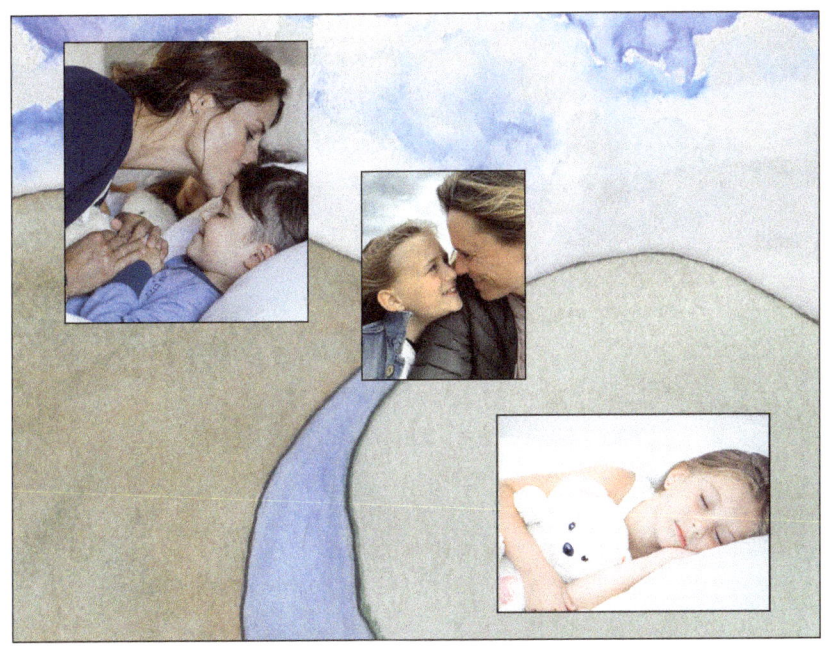

Guidance and My Sleep Course
Having trouble getting your child to sleep?
You want some help? You're not alone. So many
parents around the world are struggling to help their
children to sleep. Find more help here:

www.inmyheart.eu

More from Gitte

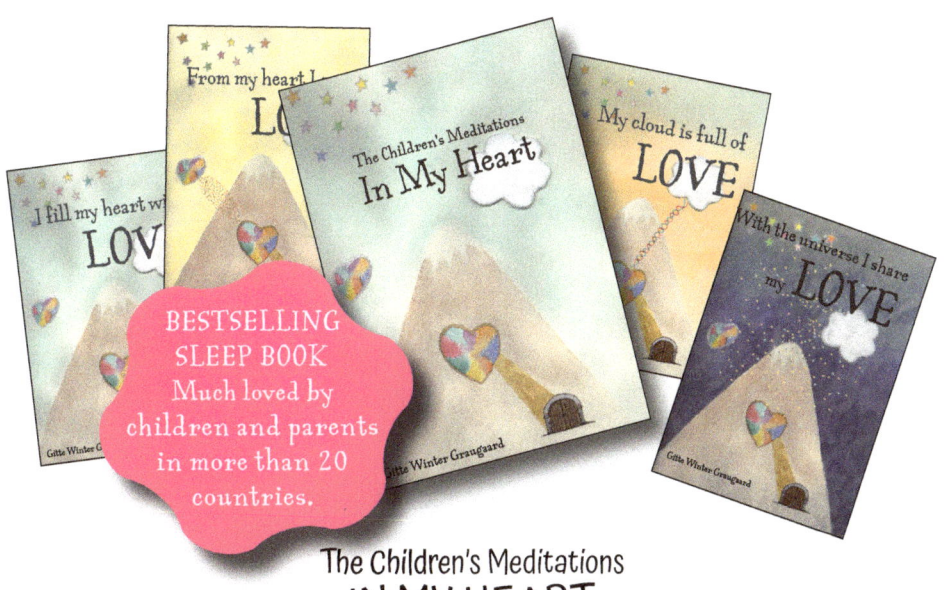

The Children's Meditations
IN MY HEART

This bestselling book is teaching thousands of children to find their
Love Mountain and fill themselves with love. It works very well with
"HEARTLIGHT". You get four amazing meditations in one book.
They also help your child to sleep and teach your child
about empathy, appreciation, connection and so much more.
Now selling in more than 20 countries in multiple languages.

www.inmyheart.eu

THE VALLEY OF HEARTS

An amazing series of books with meditations for children written by Gitte Winter Graugaard. Show your child how to reach their inner valley. "Meet Chief Eaglefeather" (no 1) and let him teach how to use the four elements: Fire, Water, Earth, and Air. Help your child cleanse their own energy with "The Flamedancers' Fire" (no 2). Cleanse off other people's energies under "The Clear Cascade" (no 3). Find peace in "The Deep Meadow" (no 4). Fly high to get new perspective on "The Mild Winds" (no 5).

www.thevalleyofhearts.com
#kidsmeditate

More from Gitte

Gitte is on a mission
to teach 1 MILLION children
to meditate. You can help her
by sharing this book and your
experiences with others. Ask for
her books at your local library,
or at your favourite bookshop and
use as presents to those you love.
Support her mission.

Thank you for teaching your child to meditate.

See you soon ...

Ingram Content Group UK Ltd.
Milton Keynes UK
UKHW051439210423
420571UK00008B/51